Polytheogamy

Polytheogamy

Poetry by Timothy Liu

Paintings by Greg Drasler

Saturnalia Books
13 E. Highland Ave., 2 Floor
Philadelphia, PA 19118
info@saturnaliabooks.com

ISBN: 978-0-9818591-0-1
Library of Congress Control Number: 2008936645

Book Design by Saturnalia Books
Printing by Westcan Printing Group, Canada

Cover Art: Lobby by Greg Drasler

Distributed by:
University Press of New England
1 Court Street
Lebanon, NH 03766
800-421-1561

The poems in this book first appeared in the following publications: *Bloom, Born, Boulevard, The Butcher Shop, Cab/Net, Call, Chautauqua Literary Journal, Chelsea, Cincinnati Review, Cream City Review, Damn the Caesars, Dragonfire, Drunken Boat, Five Fingers Review, Green Mountains Review, Harvard Review, Indiana Review, The Journal, Knockout, Lyric, Margie, Missouri Review, The Modern Review, Natural Bridge, The New York Quarterly, Octopus, Pool, Potion, Redivider, Ribot, Sawbuck, Shampoo, Slope, Typo, Ward 6* & *Witness*. My thanks to the editors for their generous eyes on these.

Contents

Reading Polytheogamy

Timothy Liu has his elegantly precise lyrical side consider "Aubade":

It was your tenderness

broke me, our secrets
spilling into the dark

of a hotel room lit up

by a clock we forgot
to set as the minutes

meandered through us

into the landscapes
seen only from a bed

floating towards dawn—

This is morning song with a difference, with an overcoming of mourn-
ing achieved by an intensely playful directness. Liu's diction is always
alive with pointed surprise. One realizes that one plausible way to meas-
ure the impact of tenderness is to recognize a capacity for the violence of
breaking through to the body—spilling secrets with semen? And then
one can see how the awakened body might register details from a per-
spective centered in the bed and arranged as a landscape. The clock they
forget to set becomes the sign of their passion, presiding over a decep-
tively complex series of related verbs that extend the landscape toward
their bodies and establish a freedom made possible by that perspective.

But such tender moments are rare in *Polytheogamy*, or, perhaps, what we typically imagine as tenderness does not run deep enough to accommodate the intricate psychological states that emerge within Liu's intense efforts at lucidity. "The Crisis," his first poem in the volume is more typical:

Unwilling to be dragged through marriages any longer.

Was equilibrium what we were ever after?

A stasis bridging the dual abyss?

Never mind that carousel on which we endlessly ride.

Hip flab hanging off forty-something hags.

Nothing sadder than a clown fingering dirty bills.

His shorts ripped off.

Rolling blackouts said to be expected all summer long.

The first line of the volume makes clear Liu's expectations of his readers. The possibility of exhilaration begins in the negative, so long as one can envision all that drives the negative. This is Liu's present tense, the tense where change is recorded and orientations redefined. This is also the space to look back, to ask (and to answer in the asking) the question whether equilibrium (presumably of marriage) was what we were ever after. But the opening to the present must retain a good deal of the negative, if only in the insistence on recognizing without illusions the various components that define the space where possibility might reign. Then in lieu of traditional lyrical fleshing out of this sense presence, Liu likes to shift perspectives—here to expectations of the future seen in an ironical move to what seems a public perspective. For Liu affective shifts in private perspective seek to make their mark on the public world, however incomplete the hold on that world. These blackouts are the spaces of freedom seen in terms of figures of space that encompass how bodies take up new permissions. Anything less comprehensive and distanced might be self-delusion providing short term satisfaction for the lovers but also producing roles that produce their own drag.

We have isolated several oddly matched elements giving Liu's poems their distinctive power—the insistence on lucidity, the work the negative does to reinforce the poetry's attachment to actual bodies and their states, the ironic fact that negation also opens a substantial place where freedom can be promised and affect intensified, and the strange ways that Liu moves by an enthematic logic that in its semantic and perspectival leaps manages to aerate the counter-thrust toward the pressure to substitute accurate names for what might satisfy conventional lyric desires. Now I want to harvest (as Anne Sexton might say) by turning to two of my favorite poems in this volume and exploring what Liu can construct with these tools. The first poem is one of the texts entitled "The Marriage":

> The wife he could no longer fuck
> was like an inflatable doll mutilated
>
> beyond repair—same mouth, same
>
> holes—until he shot a new hole
> hole into her, hoping she would fly off
>
> into space the way a child lets go
>
> of a mylar balloon at ocean's edge,
> knowing wherever it came to land
>
> would have nothing to do with him.

Negatives frame this poem—formally establishing a balance among the sonically lush details and semantically staging a movement of mind that is both disturbing and weirdly exhilarating. The first negative makes a brilliant beginning because it seems a durative form: the negative is not a passing observation about the wife but a fundamental defining quality, as if he could not look at her without being reminded of this characteristic of their lives. No wonder metaphor follows. Such surprising openings, and such disturbing feelings, need tempering and contextualizing analogies. Here the metaphor not only intensifies the pain but builds an alternative site where he can imaginatively act on his feelings, and in the process, establish a more evocative and substantial metaphoric dimension for the poem.

The metaphors lead to the perspective of the child, who in a highly compressed logic shoots a hole in the inflatable doll to release another inflated object so as to be free of it. This identification with the child however quickly ceases to be only metaphoric. The figure of the child is carried though to the final negative because through the child, the husband can fully acknowledge the significance of what it might mean to be free of the wife become intolerable object. The child can enjoy that freedom, while the poet has the deeper enjoyment of recognizing how identifying with the child flaunts all of our culture's rhetorics of maturity and of acceptance. The poet's nothing now becomes a richly substantial freedom because it includes the very ideas of maturity (or stasis) that the figure of the balloon so gleefully repudiates.

It is difficult not to think about Robert Creeley when reading Liu's sparse and unrelentingly lucid lines. Even Liu's insistently enthematic logic echoes Creeley, albeit it with an indulgence approaching but not embracing surrealism. But there are emotional timbres that even a gay Robert Creeley might not risk. Creeley's lucidity is pained, is won in a continuous struggle with silence. Liu's lucidity is ludic, or almost ludic because of his sense of the freedom evoked by his insistent refusal of lyric expansiveness. The negatives born of Liu's lucidity become strange sources of plenitude.

In "The Marriage," the emotional field is characterized by a sense of relief and, more generally, of finally being allowed to encounter a negative space from which no call to positive language need emerge. "What the Magdalene Saw" is far more effusive, offering a single sentence sonnet that arrives eventually at one crucial basic source of pleasure in subjecting the imagination to the limitations and the permissions of the senses:

> This fat cum pig more than eager to drop
> his five spot in my lap, perhaps another
> twenty in some motel-by-the-hour mopped
> up with Clorox whenever strangers spurt
>
> on thread-bare sheets to shroud a beat-up
> mattress scarred with tiny cigarette burns
> as towel-wrapped lunchtime gents line up
> outside the door—peccadilloes that turn
>
> into another unsafe orgy grope fest *sans*
> *culottes, Cheri, mais toujours avec le petit*
> *mort* said the enormous married hard-on
> looking to unload inside a room complete
>
> with real time chat, myself a dirty whore
> nailed down by some chubby bear I abhor.

Many of these poems are astonishing in their own right. But *Polytheogamy* also offers a remarkable series of images by Greg Drasler. Intricate and evocative, these images also establish a powerful dialogue with several features of Liu's style, especially the relation between negative and positive or empty and full spaces created by shifts in perspective. I wanted to call attention to a "tension" between these two kinds of force. But now I see that one measure of the power of the dialogue between this poet and this painter is how much it beggars any metaphors like "tension." "Identity" between emptiness and fullness would come closer to what they both accomplish. Yet "identity" is too theologically charged a term, and it does not sufficiently point to how the fullness is in the relations among details and so resists the piety of such conceptual model terms.

One mode of emptiness in Drasler is the apparent reduction of figures to repetitive patterns where no individuating mark seems to make a difference. This creates a pleasant shock when we parse the image and see how small differences can reconfigure the entire space. There are three luscious images of men in hats that seem at first all going in the same direction. Once we notice the differences in directions, the entire ontology of the image changes. Now there emerge not only orthogonal conflicts but the work pulsates with variations in color and the proliferation of structural units. Similarly Drasler seems fascinated by repeating forms in images of wall paper or luggage, or one of my favorites, a series of three almost identical beds and bedcovers. The color harmonies fill the room in their own right, so here one is tempted to yield to the beauty of sheer repetition. Then the eye picks up some differences quickly, like the tan hat on the yellow of one bed cover and the fishing items on the cropped bed in the foreground. These beautifully complement the color scheme. But they also call attention to the strange perspective where depth of field is established because of a view from the side rather than one stressing recession from a frontal plane. And that in turn establishes marvelous effects for the repeating elements. Trace the three stripes in the bed cover, for example. They do not only differ because of recession in space. Because the recession is sideways they seem quite independent forms—the repetition now is in the service of recognizing differences. Yet the differences are there because the shapes repeat exactly, but in emphatically different places, so placement becomes at least in part the determiner of what matters for the eye's sense of fact.

Drasler's richest images are also the most evocative in relation to Liu's writing. I cite as example the first image of an interior of a car, which becomes a richly varied motif throughout the volume. This interior is offered from a perspective at the side of the car, with no intervening structures. The viewer is already inside the near wall of the car, so the eye is greeted by empty seats drastically foreshortened, then a great illusionary continuous window that opens into vacuous washed out space. The emptiness is gradually tempered by attention to details like the two books on the back floor and the instrument panel. But the wonder is how the extended blank of the window sets the key for a series of positive absences—from the negative space within the steering wheel to the blank darker mirror on the pale bland snippet of the front windshield to the small rear side window and just a hint of the rear opening. The open space within the car that originally evokes a dramatic emptiness becomes part of a continuous blankness that is itself a domain of infinite yet perhaps empty possibility. The container is contained by echoes of itself. And the various forms become emphatically the spare content that in its spareness promises a not unproblematic plenitude.

— Charles Altieri

THE CRISIS

Unwilling to be dragged through marriages any longer.

Was equilibrium what we were ever after?

A stasis bridging the dual abyss?

Never mind that carousel on which we endlessly ride.

Hip flab hanging off forty-something hags.

Nothing sadder than a clown fingering dirty bills.

His shorts ripped off.

Rolling blackouts said to be expected all summer long.

THE MARRIAGE

As ever he'd been looking for someone to blame.

Ill-effects of hurry on the tissues.

Tiles made out of fossilized ferns installed in the vestibule.

Love duplicating the key's toothed steel.

Hence the steady decline.

Sordid ghosts caught inside the door-dwell of an Otis.

THE ACCIDENT

The gentleman reading the paper on the morning train
was not awake.
           It was clear he had stepped into his suit
while lost in the middle of a dream, a suit he hadn't
worn for over a decade,
                the boutonniere still fresh
from after the winter social when he and his friend
would take the same girl for a drive,
                    fuck her right there
in the middle of the dunes, politely taking their turns
all night long
           in the only way that they knew how
to make love to each other without shame as the girl
lay there like an intersection
                  governed by a broken
traffic light sometimes blinking off and on till dawn—
an accident he would read about
                all the mornings after.

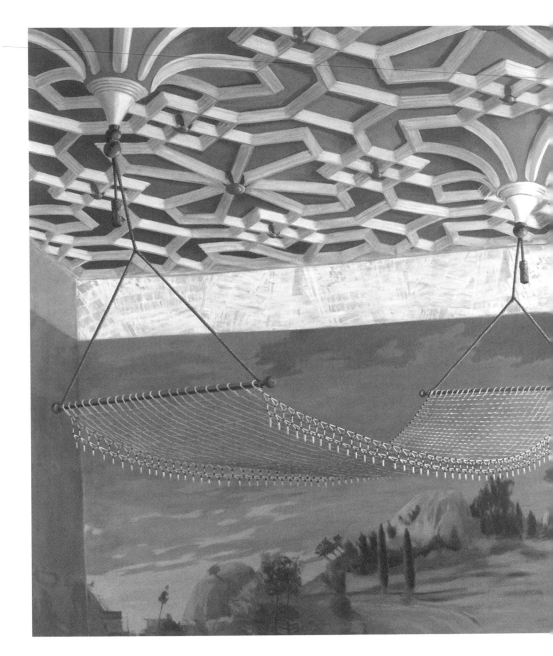

THE INVENTION

A bullet-ridden burden he set down.

A city erupting out of salt.

What he felt entitled to.

Hidden in the heel of his left shoe.

Some said the right.

Unable to entirely recall.

What this had to do with happiness.

THE MARRIAGE

The wife he could no longer fuck
was like an inflatable doll mutilated

beyond repair—same mouth, same

holes—until he shot a new hole
into her, hoping she would fly off

into space the way a child lets go

of a mylar balloon at ocean's edge,
knowing wherever it came to land

would have nothing to do with him—

TILL DEATH DO US PART

As soon as my mother left
my father, he found himself

another wife as fucked up

as the first, the one she was
meant to replace, the one

he was happy to show

on their honeymoon night
who was really in charge

as he repeatedly cried out

the name of my mother
at the moment that he came

inside his new bride, knowing

on all the nights thereafter,
she would surely know

who had gotten there first—

TILL WE BECOME UNKNOWN TO OURSELVES

Each would parent the other's wounded child.

Practiced as they were settling for less.

What widens to a keyhole.

Molotov cocktails hurled at a Hummer.

Transporting all that baggage.

Love's absurd excess.

Shipped out to the billion available channels.

ROMANCE

Had wanted to get down
to the floor of him
where tucked inside

his briefs a shameless
self-promoter wantonly

lurked—more than
eager to please and now
we were driving into

the interior, a bedroom
paneled in first-growth

wood with real lava
flowing inside lava lamps
a sure sign that this

was no waking dream—
moist sugar sequestered

in the corners of his
eyes where ant trails
scaled about the trellis

of his voice calling out
to the deaf man I had

become while seated
in a basement tuning
into his favorite station—

UKIYO-E

Chrysalis torn, the winged
Hiatus comes to

Reclaim its own

Immanence unfurling wet
Silk—no more the grub creeping

Aslant a serrated leaf but appetite

Reborn, having slept until the nuptial's
Appointed hour: one wing

Betrothed to

Another striking up the conjugal
Dance—watermelon seeds dripping with

Juice removed with a hairpin as

In the Meiji
Style.

THE ROOM

You who'd been seated on a stool
whose chipped reds had a feel of childhood
to them could not understand why

you were ever brought to this place—

not a single word spoken here, no meals
to sate your hunger and your growing thirst
robed as you were in white, so when

the women were brought into the room, all naked

except for the hoods placed over their heads,
women who'd been instructed to bend
over far enough to grab hold of their ankles

with their assholes facing you, you wept

for you knew your wife was among them,
and you had to admit it was impossible
to tell which of those contorted trembling forms

was yours—

AUBADE

It was your tenderness

broke me, our secrets
spilling into the dark

of a hotel room lit up

by a clock we forgot
to set as the minutes

meandered through us

into those landscapes
seen only from a bed

floating towards dawn—

MY NEIGHBOR'S WIFE

goes a-whoring, maxing out
five credit cards before she's found
dead in the woods—suicide note
gone soggy in the rain—a husband
having to repay the debt
for years to come, unmoored as he is
from wife—the male body
left to pleasure itself—the mind
so capable of wound, of flesh
glimpsed just hours after—ocular
proof where pupils widened
to gather such detritus in—
a clerk, a student, a girl in the park
unripe as she is though Eden
to the core—my neighbor's wife
more beautiful now than ever.

THE MARRIAGE

Tons of suicide rock hauled away
from Bridal Veils Falls—a couple's

bones embedded in the mud—water

upriver diverted to a trickle after
we had finished taking our belated

honeymoon. Such detritus floating

to the surface of a laboratory beaker
with trousers down to your ankles

nothing like that swab jammed up

my urethra—all eyes in that waiting
room fixed on the History Channel.

ROMANCE

He says he'd see me every day
if he could, as if I were

the Mona Lisa and he

squatting in a Parisian flat
a stone's throw from the Louvre,

ignorant of the fact

that there are copies
sequestered in a basement vault,

each rotated frequently lest

too much flash eat away
at the original withheld

from view, the Venus de Milo

in the next wing over
also said to be a gorgeous fake—

OTTOMAN TWILIGHT

Harems made to walk through a disinfectant bath.

Sundry foes turned belly-up to the sky.

Minarets at loggerheads over age-old gripes.

Nor submit to plaudits of the crowd.

Lifeline fused at the base of his bloody palm.

Diadem placed atop a virgin womb.

More high-maintenance than a Byzantine mosaic.

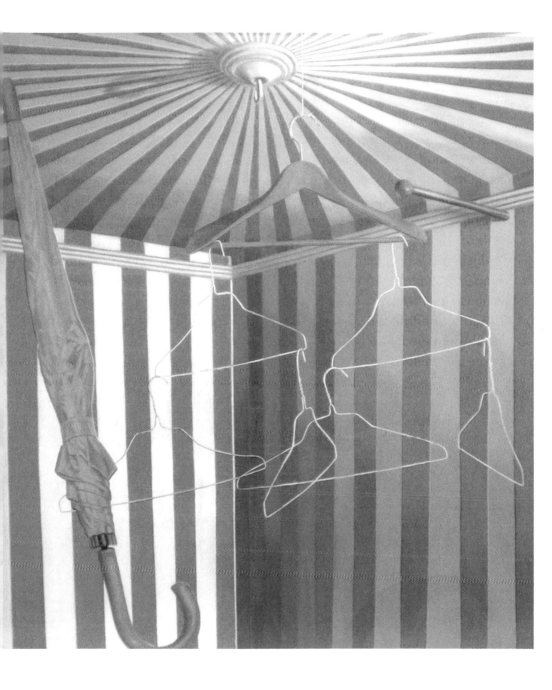

STRAIGHT UP

no matter who might

get the upper hand
over whom, having

put off disclosures

of the self, an instant
messenger lurking

in his pants at whose

expense was anyone's
guess, the martinis

coming way too fast

LIFE LESSONS

After the hour-long interview, after

inquiries into topics such as personal
vision, favorite artists, the attraction

and repulsion to schools of thought,

the master said to the star-struck lad,
"Yes! I'd like you to be my assistant.

The paltry hourly sum I offer you is

but a fraction of your worth, and yet
you do not flinch, not in the slightest.

Those who came before have added

up to nothing!, unlike you, so willing
to shoulder your fair share of shovel

scrapes." Then added, when the news

had sunk in deeper, hands escorting
our youth to the door, "One last thing—

we'll be fucking. Is that a problem?"

ROMANCE

Were the landscapes ever changing or were we?

What then was the driving force he said.

'Twas in fact the hour's toast tipping back the glass.

Entire tonal registers unsounded till his touch.

More like an itch I couldn't scratch.

Too hot as "they" say.

Collection silver spilling across the cathedral floor.

CALLED TO SERVE HIM

at whatever cost even as communion

did them in—kisses all sty and hurry
mired to archaic raunch—godly hum

pillowing boys to sleep where dreams

collapsed—love's awkward stutters
unsure of speech leveled by whispers

hand over mouth as love flooded in—

OVERHEARD IN THE BELLY OF THE WHALE

Disrupted by the opening bars.

Of earnest conversation.

The hours trimmed with fat.

With games of solitaire.

Sturdy as opposable thumbs.

This isn't Sunday School.

Or a round of Old Maid.

You've got to ante up, hear?

I'm talking inside the marrow.

THE MARRIAGE

Pushing his penis all the way up
into his body until he became

all girl. If you've seen his shit

breach ass, then you've got access
to his cookies, no questions

asked. What he said in his sleep

you said you'd better hold him
unaccountable for. *Coaxing love*

beats forcing it said the bride

deep inside. *Ask to see both sides*
of the coin before you ante up.

REVENGE WAS

almost getting

into his pants
and wanting to

bolt back home

to whomever's
eating canned

applause but no

you've got to
finish getting

him quickly off

before regret
comes to claim

what's yours—

WEDDING SONG

foisted upon us from afar the air from the Alps still fresh
on our person if not a kindness then a traditional Italian

family seated around that table longer than a tour bus

where speech-slurred phrase-book politesse filtered into
glass after glass of vintage Barolo—one yawn setting off

another till it reached upstairs between the bridegroom's

thrusts while the bride looked on in a daze as if to say
oh darling haven't we eschewed the adverb long enough

A WILD FLUTTERING

Anyone was there but it was you whose face I straddled there

underneath the clouds—roof-top pigeons with outspread wings
pinioned to a fire escape, straight or gay, you say the name and

the dream comes true, whether playing host or playing guest,

a drunken view the fools below are party to with ears laid low
all focused on the dance suspended in clockwise turns running

counter to the day's quick thrusts for some had knowledge and

some had cork, sniffed wet or dry or simply snuffed, there was
a gun or I was alone, would it matter which had gone off first?

WITH CHERUBIM AND A FLAMING SWORD

A churlish response could not disguise

nagging doubts while ministers go a-whoring
through the woods, dungeoned there

where childhoods snared to erotic servitude

rescind protected habitats. What we are
is pleasure's aftermath, a sore throat

loosening up its fiery grip when the genitals

start to run. Forget whipsnakes, fairy shrimp,
or the Mexican spotted owl—my mother

sent whistling through the seven gates

down a vortex where vast Antarctic chunks
are sheering off in ice melt not seen since

the Ice Age as runs on Cipro and Cidofovir

deplete armamentariums—all of us braced
for the next attack—strong black tea

diluted endlessly beneath a gilded samovar.

PROTHALAMION

trying to rid ourselves of the slow accumulations

stone-cold architecture one has felt by hand

the astringent idioms

wounds only childhood could inflict

however blind on the lowland path through solitude

swallowing hard the unfledged romp

no longer making hay

such deceit playing dead amidst the holiday cheer

OF THEE I SING

financial fraud all gone up for grabs

for who can stomach fossil fuel
retreating to the bedroom

where a war tribunal lodged

its shrapnel in a child's eye halfway
round the globe now drive

'twas grace that taught my heart

to fear black-iced promises,
his fractured femur jutting through

asking to be nursed back to health—

GOD SAVE THE QUEEN

She lacked passion—
not for learning
but for mouth so
shy in knowing
what it really
wanted—less a slut
than a cold beer
that settled for
the usual but mild
despair. Here comes
the sex-policed
positions. Just
hold on—let her
be more than
adequate for myth.

BECOMING MEN

He said an orgasm felt like standing
under a shower head and having

this urge to pee. Said anyone could

lose it quick by getting their hand
dipped in a bowl of lukewarm water

as they slept. Only he had gotten

pubes by then—the rest of us bald
as newborn babes. Zipped in my bag,

I tried to stay awake, accompanied

by slow refrigerator hum—afraid
that someone would make me come.

THE MARRIAGE

Tête-à-tête with loneliness, we find
ourselves unable to disentangle

from the old selves. It unshackles us
to the very site, even the poorest

among us. And the clothes we shed—
each orifice tinged with its own

perfume lingering on inside a body
that had its own intentions too.

AWOL

More chore than doling the orders out your body spent

on drills and the subtle gradations of yes giving way

to a picnic table with a pitcher of iced tea why not

cool your forehead off on an afternoon so full of June

one wants to postpone those dramas gripping down

wayward grunts doing the asphalt crawl in quonset huts

complete with bunks and a host of flies closing in

as your anger sugars over to an almost forgotten tune.

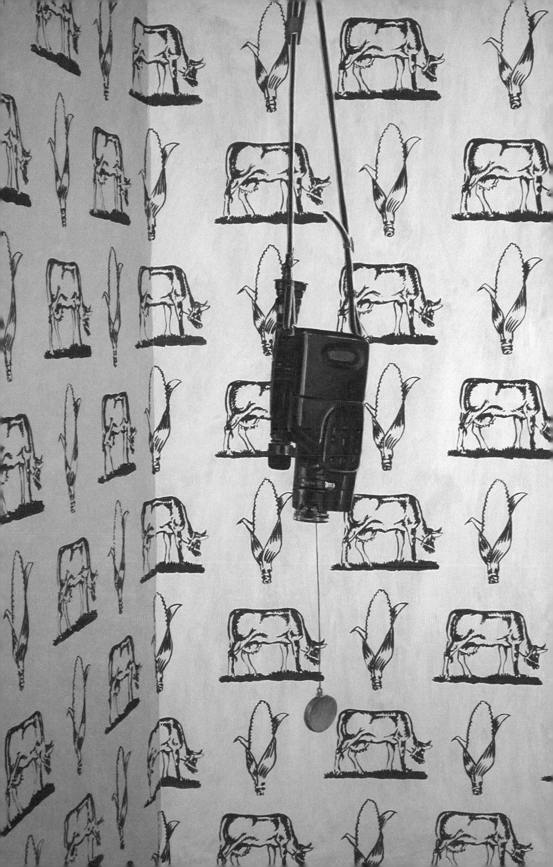

THE ASSIGNATION

Agreed to meet. To exchange
whatever else to further

the fulfillment. The ante
followed by affect's

escalation. Always met
"in public." Had asked if I was

"reckless" followed by
the usual innuendos, emails

each held onto as certain
proof, jacking off

in our separate worlds.
And who's to say we didn't

come together after all?
So many deposits left

where interest failed to accrue.

ROMANCE

He says, *I'm not in love
with you,* says, *you're*

*not the kind of man I'd
imagine wanting to*

spend the rest of my life

with—this said while
fueling up at a rest stop

with a half-smoked joint
dangling from his lips—

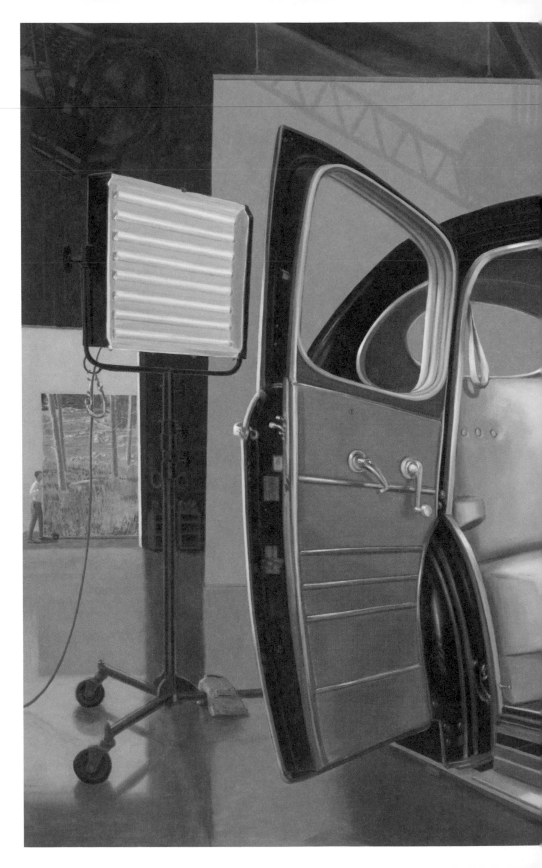

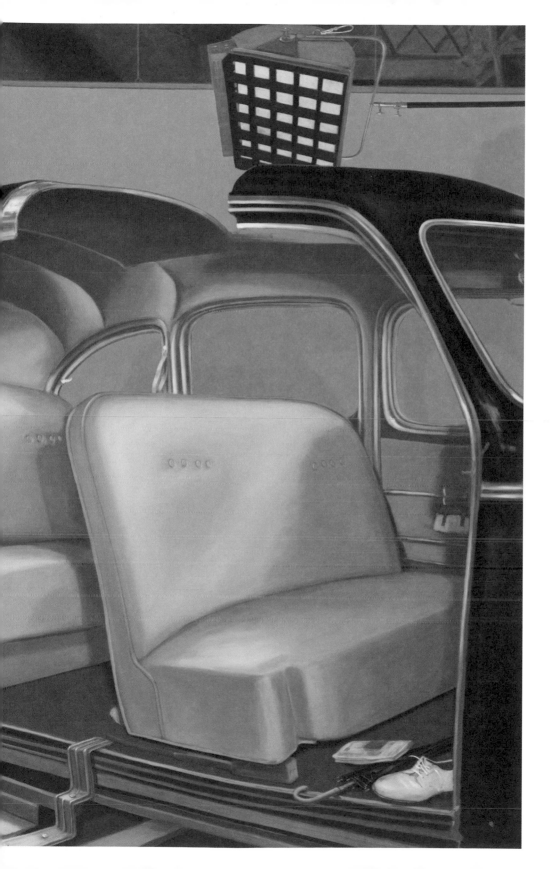

TO WOO THE NUPTIAL WOE

Our love all habit now—a jack-off fest
crudely put. And what we do we do

with practiced hearts around each other's
wants, no surprises left in the spine's

torqued requests, this way, that way,
and the house far better off than worse

with loneliness held at bay, held in arms
that want to hold the beloved back—

THE BEAUTY OF ANONYMOUS MEN

Seemingly a cure. Accustomed more
to noontime acid trips than anything

more of the depths. A year or two
enough to ravage anyone's looks—

youth's allure as balm to advancing
age where lamps along the Hudson

flicker on at dusk—manifold forms
of tenderness eluding patrol-car glare.

NO CHASER

Never mind those ready-mades lining up
         outside the club. Order Absolut. Choose
                  between an olive or a lime while waiting
         for the man to show, scent of him stronger
than memory's snare. Nothing to keep you
         safe, not even a full-body latex condom
                  from head to toe. Think how many others
         are being stood up now. *And your illness*
hardly interests me. And the trouble is
         I cannot love you as you are. Two fags
                  smoking each to each under a disco strobe
         as you survey the ceiling tin—the antique
barroom mirror permanently clouded over.

DEAD MEAT

seismic cracks spreading across plaster bison chained

to a wild oak a cloud of birds all atwitter veering

this way that way nor do we belong as chickens feed

by a barnyard trough as semis haul hot and moist

toothless mouths down interstates greased by drunken

joyride's breathalyzed nightmare oaths of blood

for once is twice as good as lost when the condom

tears oh the morning after syrupy and hickory-smoked

inside a spine-cracked diary the pages rabbit-eared

AARON'S ROD

We have no honor, save
the bodies that we give
away. A mother smiles
and a child feels exposed.
The boys who undress
in the basement of a church
beat it. At least that.

DOMA

The match sputters—
empties into my cigarillo's

dry tip, his palm-cupped
jitney eased into for
offered courtesies as my

hand's outer edge
nudges his ever

so slightly that I
think of Christ's hem
offended by a stranger's

need, a crowd of need
ministered to, one flame

alit by two outside
the café, inhalation, ex-
halated yin to

yang—entangled
smoke rising from our lips—

TILL DEATH DO US PART

In a world that won't come clean, men

still open their doors, sending most
downriver to where the gods have gone—

for who can resist cheering on unchaste

boys who ride bareback into dawn—bodies
glazed with salt that won't wash off

even if they wake up in their own beds.

THE ASSIGNATION

Our intentions were all pencil,
hardly a signature. How easily

the letters smudged—a crisis
underneath the daily rhythms

we called our lives. Scribbles
left on the edges of a discarded

grocery list. A passion born of
all the useable ravages of age—

over and over in the absence
of the other. The afternoon all

fountain and shine. No relation
to the clutter left on our desks

hinting at the other life unlived.

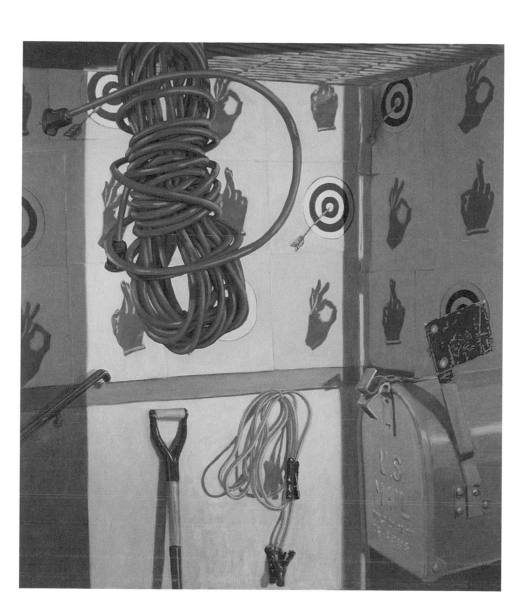

VOWS OF SILENCE

As surely as our limbs entwine, torrential
downpour rendezvous soaking through

the sheets. Where sundry wonders are up
against a durable latex sheath, forget

tonalities pulpit-chained to a mother lode
of fear. Then comes a sudden spasm

slaked with copious pearl—holy tongues
dungeoned there making a cold retreat.

THE MARRIAGE

results of chance and happenstance

tchotchkes suitcased on some carousel
held up by an airport guard

anger's intermittent toggle jostling loose

the scent of you attachéed
to an obscure embassy

your mural-like ambition hoarding space

my truck with you goat-hooved and spry

if only weather could be willed if kiss

history's peripatetic nightmare reel
in lieu of royal carpet dowry

or outposts lodged at the edge of dream

a hat check left unclaimed

with eden and maiden dungeoned there
behind such austere tropes

LIKE A DOG TO HIS OWN VOMIT

Washed in the blood of Christ, you emerge

anew but for the old blood pumping still
to reassert itself long after the novelty has

worn off. His body all verb-studded excess.

The spirit is strong but the flesh is weak!
Or was it the other way around? You can't

remember last week's sermon, only some

hell to pay—aversive therapy strapping
your dick to a chair, electrodes firing up

like bloods from the 'hood scoring joints

from a Mister Softee van, each strung out
and growing fat on violence at the local

mall till someone shoots a look your way

as if meaning to say: "The management
regrets to inform you that your patronage

is no longer appreciated." What selves

we have ceded to make our own occult
composite of regret, our icons traded-in

for ivy leaves ironed-on a frat boy's briefs.

WHY NOT

Because you don't
respond. Because

I can't submit to
actuary tables

nullifying cost.
Because emotion

lacks precision,
anxiety alone

necessitates re-
calculation. Can't

help but usher in
future's bride

instead of over's
even if. Why not

levy duty upon
desire's sure toll—

INTIMATIONS OF IMMORALITY

The sound of sleet on glass kept her up
all night, a comforter stuffed with down

slowly migrating to his side of the bed.

Had he whispered something in his sleep,
the name of another woman, or perhaps

a man? The walls so thin she thought

she heard an infant crying out for milk.
No. More like some newlyweds fucking

in a room that should have been theirs.

NO VACANCY

Had to go walkabout in the snow—a flat
the cause of his good luck as prelude to

illicit touch—a motel key left dangling

in the lock. Nothing but cool distances
would keep him coming back, branches

along that burnt-out road sleeved in ice—

a man twice his age caught in gorgeous
nakedness glimpsed through winter glass

fogged-up by a truant schoolboy's breath.

GIVE ME BACK MY MAN

Attention fashionistas! Your accouterments are neither *de rigeur* nor *echt*, caught up as we were in the cul-de-sac of a prozac dream

where late Romantic twilight looked spritzed and buffed—nipples glazed with wanton kiss as they piled on the schmooze. Such flam-

boyant effrontery got off on snowboarding hotties heading towards the slopes. Was the road to Olympic gold enough for us or was it

merely infinite tape delay?—our sex lives yet committed to a ten-episode season. He said *I'll get back to you when I get back, okay?*

LONG DISTANCE

Boosting signals through a fiber-optic cable.

To get him horizontal at any cost.

Genteel suburban villas where angle is all.

Memory framed by Bauhaus glass.

A time-share like no other.

His oral-sex technique so Byzantine.

Hazmat teams called in to contain the leak.

Nor reproduced in any catalog.

Our future strewn pell-mell across the vanity.

THE ASSIGNATION

Downloading facts. Miscellany chambered into privacy. Overdoses

jacking the price of "managed" healthcare through mansard roofs
gilded gold like any old romantic tome spammed to a lusty fuck

who just loves to chat online or off. "Very dirty," Herr Mahler said,

an actual ton of dust removed from a Paris Theater. For dreams
would only come if there were flowers in the room, lovers deep

in conversation overheard downstairs while he drifted off into sleep.

GOING BUST

Banned meat infected with mad-cow disease
on sale at the Circus Circus where just last week
a clown was caught spraying fecal matter
into the smorgasbord.
                                        Must've taken weeks for them
to nab him, & who knows where I was by then—
my platinum Seiko left on a sudsy counter
in that Winnemucca john pawned
within the hour.
                                        The last of my quarters gone
with those cherries from the "loosest" of slots
as I crawled back to a lifestyle destined
to fail out there in the suburbs
of the Wild West—

Virtuosos playing on the jawbone of an ass.

Vodka bottle open and my pants already off.

Nothing in sharp focus on that hand-held cam.

                                        Somewhere tonight
someone's being raped, & someone else gets hunted
down—helicopter searchlights coming through
the trees where all the birds are singing
because they think it's dawn.

AND THEIR SINS SHALL BE WHITE AS SNOW

The town's five baseball diamonds neatly groomed.

Verging into solipsistic terror.

Hay-loft hanky panky as the hat goes round.

With boredom at the root.

Tract homes across America approximating field.

Holiday malls strung out in Xmas lights.

Purveyors of a terra incognita.

Human travail.

Trapped in a moral hell but making beauty just as well.

TURNED AWAY

from soiled sheets

where a couple
had been reading

Dostoyevsky—M.

riding on a train
through the Alps

facing his future

foe, not yet having
seen the portrait

of the woman who

would leave him
at the altar more

than once lest she

accept all he had
to offer. Romance

is not about having

nor sitting down
at a wooden table

to a hot breakfast

where harvested
honey from a jar

sweetens all of it.

THE RIGHT TO LIFE

To ask is to receive: what else were we for
that pleasure should incline against this
stiffened thrall? Nascent legislation vetoed

off the table—fetuses sliding down that
slippery slope straight into the arms of
old maids shawled in lamb's-wool shrouds

parading after dark as if the neighborhood
were cruising for a Christ—two men
pushing a stroller with a stolen baby in it.

GOING DOWN

Flushed with wine his petaled cheeks in need of kiss.

Erotic tactics that only go so far.

Thank God for crucial errors cutting through the teleblather.

A one-night stand that would last a year.

But enough to start a brawl.

Jarring the mind out of its well-traveled rut.

A quest for healing that quickly followed on our heels.

Making way for the practiced tongue.

Ennui gone wrong.

Some heavenly voice that sailed on past our pious knees.

ROMANCE

Why in the fuck don't
you write me when I know you

still want to fuck me?

DIRTY

As wives across America settle into
rerun mode. As their frequent-flyer
husbands deplane in a podunk town—
pockets full of skin-flick brass. Hot
for dick and liking it too—world-class
poolside abs keeping me from Paul
Celan—the ashen hair of Shulamite
no match for hunky jizz. The pathos
of my being here probing a stranger's
ass—crack-stench left on a wedding
band that won't come off with soap.

STONEWALLED

clandestinely gay for decades then coming out
to no acclaim whatsoever

long afternoons in lieu of sports

modeled after nameless moods of childhood
resisting arrest en masse

analysis draining off remorse

so démodé in this era of middle-class romance
soft-pedaling one-night stands

the family portrait to be discarded at once

viral loads
shelved before the biopic shooting could begin

split-level income brackets doing them in

such need for dominance rooted
to a past-peasant life

condemned to the lowest cardiovascular run

last-pick sissies
dividing up their spoils upon the frotteur's bed

DOOM QUEENS

My student who said he felt
so "Sylvia Plath" (winding up

on a stretcher heading towards

the morgue) was in my office
just hours before with his paper

in my lap, and I wanted him

to drop the course right there
instead of my getting stoned

on his weed, laughing aloud

about Anne Sexton sunk deep
into her drink, having been

denied her Guggie once again—

WHO PUTS US OUT TO PASTURE

abandoned couch potato deprived of the news when the local judge had his cable cut

missiles televised in green night vision navy seals caught in a tide of cease and desist

his plaint all sprezzatura lacking technical finesse his body milked for lush sonorities

as prelude to illicit love or was he just another sexually-dysfunctional porn addict oh

to have been a meat-market has-been no longer looking for top billing only to bottom

EXTREME UNCTION

For lovers emptied of their kiss a dream undone.

Reduced to this old bell as sinners kneel.

Hammers breaking stone to birth the arms and lips.

Toiling today for tomorrow's bread.

His body unadorned but garment to the bride.

His bare hands world enough.

Drunk on prayer as he rode me to the nethermost.

WHAT THE MAGDALENE SAW

This fat cum pig more than eager to drop
his five spot in my lap, perhaps another
twenty in some motel-by-the-hour mopped
up with Clorox wherever strangers spurt

on thread-bare sheets to shroud a beat-up
mattress scarred with tiny cigarette burns
as towel-wrapped lunchtime gents line up
outside the door—peccadilloes that turn

into another unsafe orgy grope fest *sans
culottes, Cheri, mais toujours avec le petit
mort* said the enormous married hard-on
looking to unload inside a room complete

with real-time chat, myself a dirty whore
nailed down by some chubby bear I abhor.

ROMANCE

How else free ourselves from
what we hoped the future

might bring, the slippage hot

between us as the friction rubs
off what had been assigned

in favor of what cannot be

known. To know the difference
between flirting with the fuck

and fucking with the flirt will

cost you dearly—no other
way to know what is needed

long after the face comes off—

THE MARRIAGE

Bodily need unmet where touch surpasses want as one reverberates all day

from the unremembered dream. Monuments wanted for every passing
moment—a pigeon balanced on each bronze wing of an angel overlooking

an anonymous grave. If we die, we died with our eyes on, the romantic said.

That's how palpable all should have been on earth as in the mind. Wordless
conversations that shaped us unannounced. The two of us standing there

with dust in our throats, two freight trains uncoupled at last. As if awaiting

judgment every moment of our lives, we who had lounged in bed with voices
burning like winter sun across the sea on which we sailed. He who sings

no more once sang to me, nurtured slow on lullaby, chords of troubled peace.